Guide to the Parochial Registers and Records Measure 1978 as amended at 1st January 1993

With practical suggestions for custodians and users

CHURCH HOUSE PUBLISHING
Church House, Great Smith Street, London SW1P 3NZ

ISBN 0 7151 3747 6

First published April 1978

Second edition revised and expanded 1992

Printed in England by Orphans Press Ltd., Leominster, Herefordshire.

CONTENTS

		Page
Foreword		4
I	Introduction	5
II	Operating the Measure in the Diocese	9
III	Practical Suggestions for the Making, Care and Preservation of Records	12
IV	Records Management for Parish Officers	20

Appendices

A.	Summary of the Measure	25
B.	Schedule 2 to the Measure	40
C.	Model Directions for Bishops under Section 11(6)	42
D.	Notes on Search and Certificate Fees	44
E.	Notes on Parochial Libraries	48

FOREWORD

I warmly welcome this well-timed second edition of the official Guide to the Parochial Registers and Records Measure 1978.

Those familiar with the first edition will find that the current revision takes full account of the few, yet important, amendments to the 1978 Measure which are contained in the Church of England (Miscellaneous Provisions) Measure 1992. These are due to come into force on 1st January 1993.

There remains, however, besides legal information, a great deal of practical wisdom inherited from the earlier edition. This element, too, partly technical and partly administrative, has in some places required either expansion or revision in order to allow for new factors in the contemporary scene.

I am delighted to have this unusual opportunity, and I thank, wholeheartedly, all those who in whatever capacity, religious or secular, dedicate skill, time and energy to the care and cherishing of our parish records.

Secondly, in the specific context of this Guide, I also express my gratitude to the small working party that was appointed late in 1986 by the Standing Committee of the General Synod, and to its staff. The group was given the following three tasks: to review the first ten years' operation of the 1978 Measure; to propose any necessary legislative and administrative reforms identified by that review; and finally to bring up to date the contents of this Guide in the light of any reforms which might ultimately be approved. All three tasks have now been completed.

Thirdly I thank one individual above all – the Venerable Bazil Marsh, the chairman of the outgoing review group from 1986 to 1992 and Archdeacon of Northampton from 1964 until 1991. His wise counsel and long and distinguished service in this field – it was he who over a decade ago piloted the 1978 Measure itself through the General Synod – has earned him the Church's lasting gratitude. In company with many others I wish him every happiness in retirement.

+ GEORGE CANTUAR

I INTRODUCTION

The Need for Legislation in 1978

1 Three developments in the years leading up to 1978 had paved the way for a new Measure, updating and consolidating the law in this area of church administration. First, there had emerged a sharper appreciation of the usefulness of registers and records generally, with the practical result that parish material in particular had been put to more intensive use for research of many kinds, historical, genealogical, sociological and demographic. Second, the easier means of travel and the higher mobility of modern life had exposed all types of parish property to more risk of loss or damage. More use of registers and records meant more wear and tear; shorter periods of residence in one place meant fewer years getting to know the history and tradition of any given parish. In run-down areas the problem was of course heightened. Third, but not least in importance, had been the increase in the professional skills of conservators and the vast improvements in repository facilities in this country since the preceding Measure was framed in 1929.

2 Local authorities since 1962 have had a clear power to accommodate Church and similar institutional records within their record offices on deposit. By 1978 the concept of a diocesan record office ('DRO') had in consequence changed radically since it was given legal status by the Parochial Registers and Records Measure 1929. It no longer implied a Church-owned building, staffed by Church employees. On the contrary, practically all DROs were, as they still are, accommodated in local government record offices (mainly County Record Offices - 'CROs') by agreement between the Church and civil authorities. A few, however, were, as now, housed in privately-owned secular offices (e.g. the Borthwick Institute at York) under similar arrangements with the appropriate institutions. One of the principal aims of the 1978 Measure was to enable diocesan bishops to ensure that those services, which included excellent technical advice as well as archive facilities, were fully used by the Church in the interests of the community as a whole. What was right then holds good today and, as in 1978, the Church remains doubly fortunate in that normally DROs make no charge to depositors although the other aspects of administering the Measure (e.g. inspections) are necessarily a matter for negotiation between the individual diocese and its DRO(s). For all this assistance the Church of England must continue to be profoundly grateful.

The 1992 Amending Legislation

3 Following a review of the Parochial Registers and Records Measure 1978 by a working party appointed by the Standing Committee of the General Synod, certain amendments to the 1978 Measure have been made and these are embodied in s.4 of and Schedule 1 to the Church of England (Miscellaneous Provisions) Measure 1992, which come into force on 1st January 1993. The three main amendments to the Measure will mean that (a) all parochial registers (except post-June 1837 marriage registers) that contain an entry which has become *150 years old* must be closed if still in use, and all such registers must be deposited (unless the bishop grants exemption) in the DRO; (b) the inspection of parochial registers and records can be made to coincide with the relevant *quinquennial* inspection of the church's fabric; and (c) the *archdeacon* will be responsible for seeing that the registers and records are inspected. Hitherto the Measure provided for inspections to be carried out every six years under the responsibility of the bishop.

Duties imposed by the Measure (as amended)

DEPOSIT IN THE DRO

4 A summary of the whole Measure, including the amendments which have been embodied in the Church of England (Miscellaneous Provisions) Measure 1992, is provided in Appendix A (page 25) but a preliminary statement of the main duties imposed by it will make it easier to see the legislation in clearer perspective. S.7 of the Measure requires every bishop to provide for at least one legally designated DRO to serve his diocese. Linked with this requirement is a duty laid by s.10 upon every custodian of non-current registers and records all of whose contents are at least 100 years old to deposit them in the DRO unless specific exemption is obtained from the bishop under s.11(3) to (5). To this is now added (as indicated in paragraph 3 above) a comparable duty to deposit in the DRO all *registers* whose earliest entries are at least 150 years old, after closure where necessary; marriage registers dating from after June 1837 are excepted from this new provision.

CARE OF RECORDS IN PAROCHIAL CUSTODY

5 The standard of care which is applicable to the care of registers and records retained in parochial custody (i.e. not deposited) is spelt out in specific terms. For registers and records which are normally subject to compulsory deposit in the DRO but which have been exempted from deposit by the bishop (see paragraph 4) the regulations are set out in Schedule 2 and include the requirement that a parish must monitor the

temperature and humidity conditions in which they are kept by means of a maximum/minimum thermometer and a hygrometer. For other registers and records the bishop is required under s.11(6) to issue directions regarding their safe-keeping. To enforce these duties of care the bishop has the statutory right to order deposit in the DRO and this right is backed by the further right of recourse to the civil courts. The 1978 Measure (as now amended and as stated in paragraph 3 above) imposes a duty upon the archdeacon under s.9 to operate a system of regular statutory inspections for each parish once in every fifth year. As registers and records become older and eventually qualify for compulsory deposit in the DRO, it is for the archdeacon, or his nominee, who carries out the next inspection to ensure that they are deposited or, if exempted from deposit, cared for in accordance with Schedule 2.

PUBLIC ACCESS

6 With regard to access, the 1978 Measure in its original form made no change in the law relating to searches by members of the public in registers remaining in parochial custody, but s.l6 empowered the bishop to require (whereas previously he might only authorise) the temporary deposit of all types of records in a DRO for certain purposes and these purposes were wider than those permitted before 1979 and included research. The 1992 amending legislation has modified the right of search by allowing the custodian to confine the search to a certified photographic copy (authenticated by the custodian issuing the certificate), thus avoiding the risk of wear and tear on the original. The custodian's decision may however be opposed on grounds of inaccurate or inadequate copying and if not reversed by him may be overridden by the archdeacon if he considers the grounds of the searcher's request to be reasonable.

Intended Users of the Guide

7 As different sections of the Guide are addressed primarily to different kinds of reader, it is necessary to clarify the purposes of these sections and of their supporting appendices. Section II is primarily for the use of diocesan bishops and archdeacons: consultation with local authorities, archivists and, in some cases, organisations representing user interests, are a necessary part of their functions. Section III and the new Section IV (Records Management for Parish Officers) are addressed to the actual custodians of registers and records at parish level. Frequently individual clergy ask for authoritative advice, not merely on the law but also about the practical aspects of keeping such parish materials. In

order to meet that demand the practical guidance in Sections III and IV was compiled with expert professional help. The Guide is issued, like the first (1978) edition, under the authority of the Standing Committee of the General Synod.

8 There are also five appendices. Appendix A is the general summary of the Measure. Appendix B gives the full text of Schedule 2 to the Measure (as amended in 1992). Appendix C sets out Model Directions approved by the Standing Committee of the General Synod and its House of Bishops; these are for the guidance of bishops who are called upon to issue general directions for the purposes mentioned in s.11(6). Appendix D contains notes on the Parochial Fees Order 1992 and on the Marriage Act 1949, s.63, which are relevant to s.20 of the 1978 Measure. Appendix E deals with the history and distinct legal status of parochial libraries, which should not be confused with parochial registers and records but regarded, where they exist, as another facet of parish tradition which is equally worthy of conservation.

II OPERATING THE MEASURE IN THE DIOCESE

9 The cost of inspections required by the Measure is the responsibility of the parochial church council, but as money spent on them will not be available to meet the cost of the ministry or for other important parochial and diocesan purposes, it would seem sensible to organise the operation of the Measure on a diocesan basis, with the object of minimising costs.

10 Potentially the most expensive requirement of the Measure is that registers and records should be examined and listed by persons whom the archdeacon, after consultation with the chief officer of the DRO, believes have the necessary knowledge and experience accurately to identify and describe them.

11 The Measure, unlike the Inspection of Churches Measure, does not require a diocesan scheme to settle, among other things, the order in which inspections are to be made. It would however seem sensible, and indeed necessary if the operation is to proceed smoothly, for a five-year programme to be drawn up with parishes given their places in it to provide an even work-flow for those who have to carry out the inspections.

12 What follows is a suggested course of action designed to make for smooth and economical working of the Measure.

Suggestions for the Bishop

DESIGNATION OF A DRO

13 A bishop may designate more than one DRO, and allot an area of the diocese to each of those which he decides to designate. It is not essential that a DRO should be in a diocese which it serves. The bishop should decide to whom, if to anyone, he will delegate those functions which the Measure does not specifically require him to perform personally.

14 The bishop should decide what directions he will give to parishes. They may well be mostly in the form of the Model Directions in Appendix C, but he may want, after consultation with the DRO, to add to them directions of his own, and especially directions in connection with s.11(7) and (8) of the Measure. If they are to be printed among legal notes in the diocesan directory or a similar publication, he will have to fit them into the printing programme.

Suggestions for the Person organising Inspections

15 When making a programme for the quinquennial inspections he will find that parishes fall into a number of categories:

(i) those whose registers and records have already been listed by a competent archivist, and which have already deposited them (or at any rate those whose contents are at least 100 years old) in a DRO;

(ii) those whose registers and records have already been listed but which have retained them;

(iii) the few remaining parishes whose registers and records have not yet been adequately examined and listed. This group can conveniently be divided into:

(a) ancient parishes owning a considerable number of registers and records;

(b) modern parishes with fewer of them;

and it is expected that they will be given priority in subsequent inspections.

The best programme is likely to produce a 'mixed-bag' for each of the five years. The services of competent archivists should be distributed evenly among those parishes requiring assistance. Any programme will require the consent and co-operation of parishes. It would probably be helpful to seek the support of the diocesan synod for it, and to make sure, through deanery synods and otherwise, that parishes understand the objects and procedures of the exercise.

16 In the case of parishes in categories (i) and (ii) in paragraph 15 the inspection could be made by any person with enough knowledge and experience to recognise what is described in the definitive list. Enquiries should be made of the DRO, of local societies with special historical or archival interests and of others, to identify those within the diocese who might be suitable for approval by the archdeacon after consultation with the DRO as persons competent to make these inspections. To such persons there should be allotted groups of parishes within easy reach of their homes, in order to reduce costs. Parishes in category (iii) in paragraph 15 will require the services of a competent archivist. All parishes are urged to take special care to welcome volunteers and make them comfortable during their visit.

17 The list made and certified at the inspection is an important document. The person organising inspections, the chief officer of the DRO, and others, would find it helpful if a standard form were used and record offices usually have their own standard form. If a suitable form is not printed by some central agency, consideration should be given to the printing of a diocesan form designed for easy filing and reference, on paper sufficiently durable to survive a good deal of handling through the years. It should be arranged so that those registers and records which qualify for compulsory deposit (see paragraph 5) at the inspection can readily be identified and certified.* It should provide space for the addition from time to time of information about new registers and records, and for saying where any records which the bishop may allow to be kept elsewhere than in the parish church are located.

18 Whoever organises inspections will incur extra expenditure. The liability of the parishes would probably best be discharged by provision in the diocesan budget. Early reference to the DBF would be sensible.

19 The DBF should also be asked to decide on standard mileage rates, and, where necessary, fees, to be paid to those who make inspections. They should not be left to negotiation between them and the parishes they serve.

20 Consideration should be given to the desirability of establishing a Diocesan Books and Documents Committee to work with the DRO, perhaps on the lines of or in association with the Diocesan Advisory Committee, to advise the bishop, the archdeacons and those to whom they may delegate authority in respect of the Measure, and also parishes wanting information or advice. On occasions such as those provided for in s.16 of the Measure, the bishop might find it helpful to consult such a committee. The committee could help the archdeacon and the parishes in the difficult matter of deciding what records of their life and work should be recognised as those which should be preserved, and which could reasonably be destroyed. Such a committee could provide an important element of continuity, and could ensure that the diocese takes a proper overview of its responsibilities in respect of registers and records, liturgical books and parochial libraries.

*See further, Appendix A, para 20.

III PRACTICAL SUGGESTIONS FOR THE MAKING, CARE AND PRESERVATION OF RECORDS

21 In this section of the Guide are included a number of practical suggestions for custodians of parish registers and records.

Making, Collecting and Preserving

MAKING RECORDS

22 *Ink* The clergy are responsible for continuing the registration of baptisms, marriages and burials. The Stationery Office Record Ink advised for use in the marriage registers is recommended for use in all three registers. Do not use any felt-tip or ball-point pens which may fade and can stain, spread or deface documents. Record Ink is available from: Ecclesiastical Stationery Supplies, The Hollands Centre, Haverhill, Suffolk CB9 8PR (Tel: 0440-703303/705858).

23 *Index Books* These are of value for use with all registers especially if the original register has been deposited in the DRO, when a copy of the index book should remain in the parish for reference.

COLLECTING AND PRESERVING RECORDS

24 Parish records are, like the fabric of the church, not property at our own disposal, but entrusted to us for transmission unharmed and undiminished to our successors. Paragraphs 25 to 31 give examples of what is of permanent value and should therefore be preserved, and this subject is further developed in Section IV below.

25 *Parish registers* These comprise registers of baptisms, marriages and burials, which may begin as early as 1538; of banns, which date from 1754; and recently of preachers, services and confirmations. Registers in every category, except marriage registers started after June 1837, must be formally closed when their earliest entry becomes 150 years old.

26 If marriage registers started after June 1837 and still in use are not in a satisfactory condition, they may be officially closed and exchanged for new books for which no charge is made. The same applies to *all* marriage registers started *in* July 1837. The custodian concerned is advised to contact the General Register Office (Local Services), Smedley Hydro, Trafalgar Road, Birkdale, Southport PR8 2HH (Tel: 0704 69824 ext. 442) in these circumstances before taking any other action.

27 *Records* which should be preserved include those concerned with:

churchwardens

vestries (e.g. minutes)

the parochial church council (e.g. minutes and accounts)

the church fabric (e.g. faculties, archdeacons' certificates, plans, specifications, log-books, churchwardens' annual reports, quinquennial survey reports)

other church property (e.g. terriers and inventories)

tithes

and also Pastoral Orders and Schemes, Orders in Council, correspondence, photographs, maps, drawings and files of parish magazines. Title deeds to property must of course be preserved, and the diocesan registrar should be consulted about the arrangements for their custody.

28 The Measure applies to all records 'in parochial custody', i.e. in the custody of the incumbent or priest in charge and/or churchwardens and/or parochial church council. These include any records which relate in part to the parish's former non-ecclesiastical responsibilities for the poor and highways. Records which relate wholly to those responsibilities and are still in the custody of the persons, etc. mentioned in this paragraph should also be treated as covered by the Measure unless they are claimed by a secular local government body; if there is a dispute as to who is entitled to custody of them, it may need to be resolved by the authority designated for that purpose by the Local Government Act 1972 (normally the County Council, but the Secretary of State in the case of metropolitan districts, London boroughs and the City of London). In every case of such a dispute the diocesan registrar should be consulted at the outset.

29 Records relating to charities (including church schools) should also be preserved. Where the trustees were or are the incumbent or priest in charge, churchwardens or members of the parochial church council, but in their individual and not their official capacity, or where the trustees also include other persons, it is thought that the records will not be within the Measure; they should be preserved, but kept separate from ordinary parish records, and the trustees' solicitors should be consulted about the arrangements for any title deeds to property held by the trustees.

30 Most parish records are the joint responsibility of the incumbent and parochial church council. Where there is any doubt as to whether a record should be preserved, the DRO should be consulted.

31 Some parishes possess old printed books no longer in use which may, however, still be of historical interest (Bibles, prayer books, hymn books, music and prescribed books such as the Homilies). These may be neither parish records as defined in the Measure nor a 'Parochial Library' for which there is other statutory provision (see Appendix E). The DRO may accept certain books on deposit, and if books are finely bound, they may well be of more than historic interest. None should be thrown away without consulting the Diocesan Books and Documents Committee or if there is no such Committee, the Diocesan Advisory Committee. The Council for the Care of Churches is also a useful reference point.

THE STORAGE OF RECORDS

32 The Measure lays down specific conditions for the storage of registers in which the earliest entry is at least 150 years old and of both registers and records all of whose contents are at least 100 years old (Schedule 2, see Appendix B). It also provides that the bishop shall issue directions for the care of all other records. A set of Model Directions for the use of bishops is provided in Appendix C. These can be adapted if necessary to meet local needs. In most dioceses such directions are produced by the bishop in conjunction with the chief officer of the DRO. See also paragraph 35 below.

33 Under the provisions of Schedule 2 records have to be kept in a particular type of storage cabinet or muniment room within the appropriate church. Where a cabinet is used for storage it should stand in a place as safe as possible in the event of flood or fire *and* be one which is well ventilated and likely to remain dry and in which the temperature is unlikely to vary greatly during any period of 24 hours. There should be a minimum 6 inches of airspace all round the cupboard, including 6 inches (ventilated) between it and the floor. It should not be exposed to sunlight or direct artificial heat.

34 Advice on the construction of a storage cabinet to meet these specific conditions of security, as well as the permitted variations in the ranges of temperature and humidity, can be obtained from either the DRO or the Council for the Care of Churches (83 London Wall, London EC2M 5NA; Tel: 071-638 0971). A number of parishes have installed

muniment rooms in the past and these should be designed to meet as far as practicable the specifications of BS 5454, which is the standard for record repositories. Any parish contemplating the construction of a muniment room should seek advice at an early stage from both the DRO and a qualified architect. Schedule 2 provides only for the long term storage of records; parishes retaining records subject to the Schedule may also wish to make arrangements for exhibition and research in the parish and they are strongly advised to seek the advice of the DRO in either event. If records are to be exhibited they need to be displayed in secure cases and for no longer than one month at a time. In no circumstances should records ever be exhibited or made available for research within a muniment room, the sole purpose of which is to provide storage for records.

35 There are less stringent requirements for the keeping of registers and records with entries or contents less than 100 years old (other than those registers whose earliest entry is at least 150 years old – see paragraphs 3(a), 4, 5, 25 and 32 above). However, the Measure envisages that parishes will make sensible arrangements for their storage; diocesan inspecting officers will pay particular attention to those arrangements and will advise bishops to require parishes to deposit such records if the arrangements for storage are found to be defective. Records should not be kept in cupboards or filing cabinets, nor in containers without secure locks. Safes or secure document chests are always to be preferred, and the room in which they are placed should also be kept locked. Rooms which are known to suffer from extremes of humidity and/or temperature should not be used for the storage of records, nor should those without adequate ventilation. There should also be adequate protection against fire. Although the Measure does not, except where storage conditions are unacceptable, require the records covered by this paragraph to be deposited in a DRO, in practice many parishes do deposit such records no longer required for administrative purposes, and this approach is to be encouraged.

Storing, Protecting and Repairing

'DO'S AND DON'TS' IN STORING DOCUMENTS

36 Taking trouble from the beginning will yield all the advantages of a 'stitch in time'. Among practical suggestions are the following:

(a) Do not place documents at the level of the ground, or where leaking water pipes could cause damage. If the area is prone to floods, store well above the known highest flood level.

(b) Check that all electrical circuits have been tested during the last two years. Keep a carbon dioxide fire extinguisher nearby. Use a liquid fire extinguisher only in the last resort.

(c) Make sure that documents are protected from immediate contact with metal, in cupboard walls, shelves, trays and the like.

(d) Keep documents free from dust, grease and other foreign substances. Do not store with candles, wafers, wine, ink, oil, grease or articles made of cloth.

(e) Pack documents loosely. If tightly packed, insect infestation and physical damage may result. Loose documents should be put first in boxes of archival quality, about which the DRO may be able to advise. Make sure that books placed upright on shelves are firmly supported, if necessary by rigid shelf dividers.

(f) Never keep documents in plastic bags. They prevent the vitally necessary circulation of air. The one and only exception to this rule is the strictly temporary storage in the situation described in paragraph 37(a).

(g) Avoid metal that can rust in all clips, pins, staples, tags and containers. Rust destroys documents. Brass, plastic or other non-rusting paperclips can be obtained. When tying bundles use white tape rather than string, and string rather than rubber bands, which perish and damage paper. Wrap bundles in strong white paper before tying. The DRO can advise on currently available suppliers.

PROTECTION AND REPAIR

37 (a) If the documents are in a bad condition, or in case of damage by fire or flood, get in touch with the DRO as soon as possible, where they can be repaired. Protect weak documents first with white blotting paper, and then place them within stouter covers. Do not bring any stiff material into immediate contact with a fragile document. Do not attempt to dry sodden documents. Store them in a plastic bag in a domestic freezer if no immediate advice is available from the DRO.

(b) Do not attempt any type of repair yourself. Repairs need to be carried out under the direction of those with professional expertise. Materials likely to be at hand, such as bought gum or glue, and the transparent self-adhesive strips intended for packages and parcels, and also said to be suitable for repairing printed books, *must not* be used on any documents, for they themselves in time cause irremediable damage. Natural decay can often be arrested, and, in part, made good by a trained document repairer: to patch with these materials can destroy the original beyond repair.

(c) If a document is damp and smells of mould, place it in a natural current of dry air. Seek advice as soon as possible, as the mould may still be active.

(d) When wax or shellac seals require protection, use cotton wool wrapped in polythene. Do not place cotton wool in immediate contact with wax or shellac seals; it will cause them to crumble. Interleave documents bearing applied seals with white blotting paper to avoid pressure.

(e) Some of the older parish records may be bound in leather. Leather dressing should not be used on the leather binding of a manuscript volume except after consultation with the DRO.

Making Documents Available

38 S.20 of the Measure deals with the production of registers and in certain cases, photographic copies for searches. The following guidelines may be found helpful in the case of all registers and records.

EXAMINATION OF RECORDS

39 (a) Custodians must be prepared to allow searchers, who may be genealogists, population historians (demographers) or local historians to consult the records on request, but these searches should be by appointment at a reasonable time, that is during normal office hours, or at a time outside office hours that suits both parties.

(b) It is lawful and in normal circumstances sensible to withhold production of the original of a record as long as you can offer in its place a sufficiently accurate and legible photographic copy certified by the custodian of the original as a true copy. (See the new s.20(3A)-(3C) of the Measure.)

(c) To avoid blots and smudges which can obscure the original text, make sure that no person consulting original documents uses anything but pencil.

(d) Make sure that no person using documents eats, drinks or smokes while at work, and that the notebook or writing paper is not put on the document. The use of tracing paper can damage older records.

(e) If a search is likely to be extensive, or if a competent person offers to make transcripts, temporary deposit in the DRO should be considered. The photocopying or microfilming of older records should always be carried out under the supervision of the DRO.

SECURITY

40 (a) No searcher should be left unattended. *Make no exception.*

(b) Never lend any document to an individual to take away. Once a document is in a private house, even the parsonage house, the likelihood of eventual damage or loss is much increased. If a request is made for your registers and records to go on exhibition outside the church, consult the chief officer of the DRO before doing anything. (See ss.16 and 17 of the Measure.)

(c) Try to ensure that in any case where a present or former church office-holder leaves the parish or dies no records which belong or are of historical interest to the parish are lost or destroyed as a result of the move or the winding up of his affairs.

(d) Keep a record of who has the key to every container in which registers and records are kept.

(e) Remember that Schedule 2 to the Measure relating to conditions of storage, together with the guidelines for access in paragraphs 38 to 40 above, continue to apply even while the registers and records covered by that Schedule are temporarily kept in some room set apart for exhibition or research purposes. (See paragraph 34.)

PHOTOCOPYING AND TRANSCRIPTION

41 The early registers are often the only record of local baptisms, marriages or burials, and are the documents most liable to be damaged by over-use. The best way to preserve registers is to have a microform or other photographic copy made which can be used in place of the original, provided this can be done by a photographic process which does not damage the registers. Photocopying, especially of volumes which are large, fragile or have vulnerable bindings, should be avoided. An indexed transcript is also valuable in saving the original from wear,

and ideally should go up to at least 1837, the year when civil registration of births, marriages and deaths commenced. Any competent person known to your DRO who offers to make such a transcript should be encouraged, subject to the safeguards above. Any copy made should preferably include such variant readings as may be found in any existing transcript of that register. At one time the incumbent was required to send to the diocesan registrar a transcript of entries made in the preceding year. Where they exist, these contemporary records often fill in any gaps in the original registers and are usually deposited in the DRO.

IV RECORDS MANAGEMENT FOR PARISH OFFICERS

What to Keep

42 When the majority of older parish registers and records have been deposited in the DRO, most parishes will only be responsible for records of current administrative value. Many of these will be of little or no historical value. Some, however, will be. The purpose of this section of the Guide is to give further guidance to parish officers on what records ought to be kept and what may be safely thrown away when they are no longer required for administrative purposes. For ease of reference records have been grouped into separate subject categories.

CHURCH SERVICES

43 All registers of baptisms, marriages and burials need to be kept permanently. So do the registers of banns, confirmations and services. It is strongly recommended that parishes keep an archive copy of any orders for special services or any surveys of church attendance. There is no need to keep baptism certificate counterfoils, or copies of burial certificates.

CHURCH BUILDINGS AND PROPERTY

44 Churchwardens are required by the Care of Churches and Ecclesiastical Jurisdiction Measure 1991 (expected to come into force on 1st March 1993) to compile and maintain (in the form recommended by the Council for the Care of Churches) a terrier and inventory and a logbook giving details of alterations, additions and repairs to and other events affecting the church or the articles or land belonging to it, and containing a note of the location of any other relevant documents. The churchwardens must send a copy of the inventory to the person designated by the bishop as soon as practicable after it has been compiled, and must notify that person of any alterations at intervals laid down by the bishop. The terrier and inventory and the logbook must be produced by the churchwardens to the parochial church council at the beginning of each year, together with a signed statement to the effect that the contents are accurate.

45 Previous terriers, inventories and logbooks should be retained, as should faculties, archdeacons' certificates under the pre-1991 legislation, and accompanying papers, photographs, plans, drawings, etc. Plans, correspondence, accounts and photographs relating to major repairs or alterations should also be retained. Many parishes keep or have in the

past kept a logbook or scrapbook recording parish events over the years and these are very valuable records for ecclesiastical and social historians. It is strongly recommended that all parishes maintain some similar type of document, and the form of logbook published by the Council for the Care of Churches allows space for this.

PARISH ADMINISTRATION

46 The core documents are the minutes of the parochial church council and its committees. If these are no longer written by hand in bound volumes, it is important that the signed copies of minutes are properly kept. Pasting or sticking typed copies in bound volumes is not recommended because of the generally unsound archival quality of glues and adhesives. Care must be taken, too, with ring binders because of the metal parts (see paragraph 36(g)). Loose minutes should either be properly bound into volumes or kept in an archival quality box, in which case the pages should be consecutively numbered.

47 An archive copy of all parish magazines should be kept. An archive copy of the weekly notice sheets should be kept if the parish does not produce a parish magazine or if the weekly notice sheets contain information of long-term interest.

48 Correspondence relating to routine parish administration need not be kept, but letters or reports relating to major developments in a parish should be retained if they contain important information. Parishes should retain an archive copy of replies to questionnaires or of important circulars and should also retain any statement as to the conditions, needs and traditions of the parish (a 'parish profile') produced by the parochial church council under the Patronage (Benefices) Measure 1986 on a vacancy in the benefice, as well as other documents held for or on behalf of the parochial church council or churchwardens in relation to the vacancy and the appointment of the new incumbent. Other examples of important documents which should be kept are maps of the parish specially prepared for church purposes, church electoral rolls, and parish audits. All documents should be dated.

PARISH FINANCE

49 Most parishes generate a considerable quantity of financial records, but not all of these need be kept permanently. The annual accounts of all parochial church council funds should be retained in perpetuity. (The Central Board of Finance has produced a parish account book entitled *Parochial Church Accounts*, in a loose-leaf format which provides for

the inclusion of audited accounts; full details can be obtained from Church House Bookshop.) Other supporting documents, including cash books, bank statements, wages records, vouchers and routine correspondence should be kept for at least seven years. Planned giving and covenant records should be retained for at least seven years after the end of the covenant.

PARISH ORGANISATIONS

50 Where separate organisations in a parish maintain their own records the general guidance given in paragraphs 46-49 above should be applied.

OTHER RECORDS

51 In many parishes the clergy will keep records dealing with pastoral matters many of which are likely to be highly confidential. It is recommended that in such cases a careful selection of such material be retained but that if it is deposited in the DRO it should not be made accessible until a reasonable period has elapsed from the events described. The exact period should be determined by the incumbent of the parish in consultation with the DRO. The same applies to confidential papers regarding the selection of any new incumbent for the parish.

52 In most cases the parish records fall clearly into a category in which they either have to be retained or may be destroyed after they have ceased to be current. However, there is a small number of records where historical value is limited but the bulk is considerable. In such cases it is permissible to retain a representative sample of the records, the sample to be determined by the parish in consultation with the DRO. Examples of such records are public notices, rota duty lists, offertory accounts and preliminary drafts of minutes or accounts. If it is considered desirable to sample such records, or to include within such a sample the routine correspondence and vouchers recommended for eventual destruction in paragraphs 47-48 above, then the basis for the sample must be determined at the outset and rigidly adhered to. A good basis for sampling is to keep all records in the sample categories for a fixed period, e.g. one month in every year, or one year in every ten. Where doubt exists the DRO will be able to advise.

The Computer in the Parish

53 One development which deserves mention is the increasing use of computers in the production of parish records. Typically, these are personal computers (PCs), owned by the incumbent, the parish or a

member of the congregation, and operating standard word-processing or database packages. The assistance such systems can give, particularly in larger parishes, can be very considerable, and we should not wish to discourage their use for record-keeping purposes. However, it might be helpful to touch upon two aspects which have general relevance.

DATA PROTECTION

54 The first, which is of immediate concern, relates to the Data Protection Act 1984. Briefly, the Act seeks to regulate the use and disclosure of personal information stored in computer-processable form. It applies only to data concerning living persons. Persons or organisations keeping such data are normally required to register with the Data Protection Registrar, and must as a general rule disclose to any enquirer all data they hold directly relating to that enquirer. There is a number of exemptions from all or some of the provisions of the Act, but such exemptions are strictly defined, and are easily nullified. For example, the Act appears to exempt personal information required purely for keeping parochial electoral rolls on the grounds that such information has to be published by law. However, if computer-stored electoral roll details are used for any other purpose, such as fund-raising, the exemption is lost.

55 It should be emphasised that the Act is quite complex, and many of its provisions have not yet been tested in the courts. For the time being, the best advice is: if in doubt, register. The current (1992) charge for registering is £75.00 for a period of up to three years. General information about the Act can be obtained from the Office of the Data Protection Registrar, Springfield House, Water Lane, Wilmslow, Cheshire SK9 5AX. For up-to-date information as to how the Act might affect the administrative functions of parochial church councils, it is advisable in the first instance to get in touch with the diocesan office.

LONG-TERM STORAGE

56 The second aspect concerns the longer-term problems of storage of computer-generated data. There is at present no general agreement on how long a floppy disk or magnetic tape will retain information. There is, however, agreement that much depends on the conditions in which such magnetic media are stored. Dust, smoke, magnetic fields, poor stacking and extreme temperatures can all lead to loss of data, as many computer users will have discovered to their cost. Even where storage conditions are perfect, a poor-quality disk or tape may not retain data for the three- to four-year period that, typically, material such as the records

of building work or financial transactions requires. Leading manufacturers of disks and tapes currently claim that, properly stored, their products will stay good for 'a very long time'. The lesson seems to be that if people use good-quality media of recent manufacture and, most importantly, store them properly, medium-term archiving on disk is a reasonable proposition.

57 In future, optical disks (close relations of compact disks) will probably provide a good long-term archiving medium, but at present their cost and complexity put them out of reach of parishes.

58 For the present, the safest option is to make a 'hard copy', i.e. a paper print-out, of data likely to be needed long-term. It is important to use good quality paper and to consider the conditions under which the print-outs are stored. As far as paper quality is concerned, the considerations are the same as for any paper: use the best that can reasonably be afforded. Avoid, if possible, paper containing a high percentage of woodpulp (e.g. newspaper) or any other with a high acidic content. Suppliers are normally able to advise on suitable grades of ordinary and continuous stationery. If in doubt, the DRO may be able to advise. Although paper quality is important for long-term use, proper storage conditions are crucial. These have already been discussed elsewhere in the Guide (see paragraphs 32-36).

AVOIDANCE OF ACCIDENTAL ERROR

59 When considering computer-processed records, it is worth remembering that the main cause of information loss is likely to be operator or system error (e.g. the accidental erasure or over-writing of a file, or a hard-disk failure) rather than failure of the archiving medium. The maintenance of good back-up procedures is strongly recommended.

Section of the Measure

APPENDIX A

Summary of the Measure

(As amended where indicated by the Church of England (Miscellaneous Provisions) Measures 1978 and 1992. The date of coming into force of the 1992 amendments is 1st January 1993 – see paragraph 45.)

Interpretation

1 Although this summary of the Measure follows the sequence of its twenty-nine sections and four schedules it will be an aid to clarity if certain key technical terms defined in s.25 are mentioned first.

2 *Register books* (here abbreviated to 'registers') are 25(1)*
defined as registers of baptisms (public and private), con- 6(1), 1(1)
firmations, banns of marriage, marriages, burials or services (i.e. of public worship). These are the six types already necessary for each parish under Statute or Canon Law. *Records*, on the other hand, while not including registers as defined above, means any other 'materials in written or other form setting out facts or events or otherwise recording information'. This definition is also used in the Local Government (Records) Act 1962 and will include, for example, maps, architects' drawings, photographs, lithographs, etc. The phrase *in parochial custody* differs in meaning according to whether it refers to registers or records. For registers it can only mean in the custody of an incumbent, a priest in charge or the churchwardens but in the case of records it also means in the custody of the parochial church council, and includes joint custody by more than one of these categories (e.g. incumbent and churchwardens). A definition of *burial,* added by the 1992 Measure, provides that any reference to burial also applies to the disposal of cremated remains.

Registration of Baptisms and Burials

3 Sections 1 to 5 concern the registers of baptisms and 1-5 (2,3 and
burials only. They replaced as much of the corresponding 5 as
sections of the Parochial Registers Act 1812 as were still of amended)

*As amended or added by the 1992 Measure.

Section of
the Measure

practical effect in 1978 and derive in part from them. The registration of banns of marriage and of marriages continues to be governed by the Marriage Act 1949 and is therefore not dealt with in this Measure. That of confirmations and services is still left to be regulated by Canon only (Canons F11 and F12).

4 A register of baptisms must be provided for each 1(1)(2)
parish by the parochial church council. This applies even if there is no parish church (e.g. where in accordance with s.29 of the Pastoral Measure 1983 another building serves as the only place of public worship). Where there is more than one parish church, a register must be provided for each of them. A burials register must be similarly provided unless the parish has no burial ground in use; if the parish has more than one burial ground in use, a register must be provided for each of them. Even where a parish's burial ground has been formally closed, a burial register will still be needed if the interment of cremated remains is to take place there (see paragraph 6).

5 The printed format of the registers differs very 1(3), 2(1), 3(1)
slightly from that required in the 1812 Act; and that Sched.1*
required for the burial register by the 1992 Measure differs in minor respects from the format prescribed in the 1978 Measure. Three new columns are provided in the burial register, one for the date of death, one for the date of disposal of cremated remains, and one for a churchyard plan reference number. Any registers already provided before the coming into force of either the 1978 or the 1992 Measures can still be used though it is necessary to adapt the existing books so as to take in certain additional information.

6 As a general rule every baptism or burial service 2(1), 3(1)
conducted in accordance with the rites of the Church of England must be recorded in the appropriate parochial
baptism or burial register. For the purposes of registration 25*
the term 'burial' includes the interment of cremated remains (see paragraph 2). (Funeral services which are not

*As amended or added by the 1992 Measure.

Section of
the Measure

followed by a burial registered in the parochial burial
register - for example, those where the interment takes
place in a local authority cemetery (see below) - should be
recorded in the register of services). Exceptionally, where 5*
baptisms or burials take place in certain places which do
not 'belong to a parish' but nevertheless have their own
church or chapel registers, the registration is to be made in
the appropriate register in that place. As from the coming
into force of the 1992 Measure the same exception applies
to any institution (school, hospital, etc) within a parish
which is furnished with its own registers, but not necessarily its own private chapel, and which is served by a
chaplain licensed to the institution under the Extra-
Parochial Ministry Measure 1967 (see paragraph 10). A
further exception concerns burials in certain cemeteries 3(4)
owned or maintained by secular authorities but situated
within an ecclesiastical parish. The registration of these
burials is governed by Acts of Parliament that provide for
each cemetery to keep its own register (Cemeteries Clauses
Act 1847, Local Government Act 1972).

7 Normally whoever officiates at a baptism or burial 2(1)(5)
according to the rites of the Church of England is re- 3(1)(5)
sponsible for recording it in the appropriate register. (The Sched. 1
Measure recognises that a lay person may in certain cases
be authorised to perform the ceremony and therefore to
register it.) In the following three instances, however, an
incumbent or priest in charge is the person always required
to effect registration (even though he has not officiated at
the ceremony) and to make the entry in his parochial
register. First, in the case of baptism only, he must do so 2(2)(3)*(4)
where the ceremony has taken place elsewhere than in the (5)
parish church (but still within the area of his parish) and is
not registrable in a non-parochial register (see paragraph 6)
and where the person who officiated is not a team vicar of
that benefice or a curate of the parish. Baptisms in
daughter churches, private chapels and institutions which
do not have their own registers are affected by this
procedure. Secondly, where a burial takes place in the 3(2)*(3)(5)

*As amended or added by the 1992 Measure.

Section of the Measure

burial ground of an institution to which a chaplain is licensed under the Extra-Parochial Ministry Measure 1967 (e.g. a school, hospital, etc), and where (unusually) that burial ground has no burial register of its own, the incumbent or priest in charge of the parish in which the institution is must record the burial even if he did not himself officiate. Thirdly, the appropriate incumbents or priests in charge must also record any baptisms and burials which are performed in extra-parochial places which do not have their own registers. (These places are relatively few in number and the dioceses concerned will need to refer to the Measure itself if a baptism or burial is likely to occur in one of them.) In all these cases the person performing the ceremony must as soon as possible send the incumbent or priest in charge a certificate giving details of when and where the ceremony was performed and the other particulars for registration. 2(3)*(4) 3(2)*(3)(5)

8 The Measure specifies the following form of additional entry to be entered in a register by the incumbent or priest in charge who has not performed the baptism or burial himself: 'According to the certificate of...received by me on the...day of...'. 2(4), 3(3)

9 The authorised procedure for correcting a mistake in a register of baptisms or burials (previously found in the Forgery Act 1830) is re-enacted in the Measure with minor amendments. By following this procedure an incumbent or anyone else responsible for registration under the Measure may avoid any risk of rendering himself liable to prosecution under the Forgery and Counterfeiting Act 1981. The correction must be made and attested in the prescribed manner so that legal advice should be sought by anyone not familiar with the procedure. 4

10 Section 5 of the Measure refers to certain non-parochial registers of baptisms and burials. So far as possible the Measure applies the above requirements of the Measure to cathedrals and collegiate churches, and to any other churches and chapels (with their burial grounds) 5*

*As amended or added by the 1992 Measure.

Section of the Measure

which for historical reasons do not 'belong to any parish'. This includes not only Royal Peculiars and other extra-diocesan or extra-parochial places but also proprietary chapels within the area of a parish. The same provisions apply under the 1992 Measure to institutions (with or without chapels) for which a clerk in Holy Orders (i.e. a chaplain) is licensed under the Extra-Parochial Ministry Measure 1967 to perform any offices or services.

11 While the Measure does not deal with fees for registration it should be borne in mind that church fees are prescribed in the current Parochial Fees Order for certified 20
copies of entries in baptismal and burial registers and for burials in churchyards and, in certain circumstances, in cemeteries and crematoria.

Custody of Registers in Parochial Custody

12 The Measure provides that responsibility for custody 6
of all six types of parochial register (see paragraph 2 above) rests with the incumbent or, during a vacancy, with the churchwardens except where presentation is suspended in which case the responsibility rests with the priest in charge. These provisions do not apply to a register while it is deposited in the DRO (see below).

Diocesan Record Offices (DROs)

13 The 1978 Measure requires that there is one DRO, 7(1)(2)(3)
designated by the bishop in writing, for every diocese or part of a diocese. The bishop has power to designate an existing record office as the DRO but is restricted to 7(4)
choosing a local authority repository or a place recognised under the Public Records Act 1958 or one which in his judgment is suitable as a place of deposit under that Act. Where such a record office is designated as the DRO the agreement of the authority responsible for it must be obtained first. Notice of the instrument of designation must 7(5)
then be given to the diocesan synod by the bishop.

14 The functions of DROs are mainly dealt with in later 8
paragraphs (18-21) but mention should be made of the fact

Section of the Measure

that DROs can be authorised by the Master of the Rolls to act as repositories for manorial documents and certain tithe documents formerly in parochial custody. All these are subject to statutory control by the Master of the Rolls under Acts of Parliament.

Preservation and Care of Registers and Records in Parochial Custody

INSPECTION

15 A requirement of the Measure (as amended) is that a periodic inspection of all registers and records in parochial custody must be arranged by the archdeacon. This is mandatory. The person to carry out the inspection will be appointed by the archdeacon after consulting the chief officer of the DRO. Future inspections are to take place within five years (not six years as under the 1978 Measure) after the preceding inspection has been completed. The first was due for completion by 1st January 1984 and the second within six years of the first. Exceptionally the third inspection need only take place within six (not five) years after the second if the latter was completed more than five years before this new provision takes effect (i.e. if the second was completed before 1st January 1988). 9(1)* 9(2)* 9(3)* and 1992 Measure s.4(2)

16 The detailed procedure to be followed at each inspection is left to each diocese but the following are essential elements:

(i) a full list of current and completed registers as at the first inspection; 9(5)*

(ii) a full list describing the records of whatever date; 9(5)*

(iii) a certificate of the continuing accuracy of any of the previous lists as at each subsequent inspection apart from any amendments specified in the certificate (e.g. designation of items deposited in the DRO); 9(6)*

(iv) a report on the contents of (i)–(iii) above, to be made to the archdeacon or any other person designated by him; 9(4)*

(v) the sending of copies of each new certificate to the archdeacon, the DRO, the incumbent or priest in 9(8)*

*As amended or added by the 1992 Measure.

Section of
the Measure

charge and the parochial church council (but no longer to the bishop); copies of original lists and earlier certificates should already have been sent or passed on to the same recipients.

17 The custodian of any registers or records is bound to 9(7)
make them available for the periodic inspection and the
parochial church council is liable for any expense involved 9(9)
(unless the diocese has made other provision). The council in future must also insert in or annex to the parish inventory copies of the documents sent to it (see paragraph 16) and must record the date(s) of the inspection in the parish logbook.

CLOSURE OF OLD REGISTERS

18 A new provision added to the Measure in 1992 is of 9A*, 10(2)
considerable importance but especially to custodians who already hold registers (other than marriage registers) in which the earliest entry is 150 or more years old. All such registers must be immediately ciosed if still in use, and as a general rule (see paragraph 20) must be deposited in the DRO. The same rule applies to all younger registers (other than post-June 1837 marriage registers) when they become 150 years old. The reason why post-June 1837 marriage registers are excluded is that they form part of the secular system of marriage registration to which amendments cannot be made without government legislation which may also affect both state registers and church registers belonging to other denominations. However, no *current* marriage register can date back earlier than 1st July 1837 and any worn-out current marriage register, of whatever subsequent date, may be *exchanged*, on application to the General Register Office, for a new register free of charge (see paragraph 26 in Section III of the Guide). Other
registers (baptismal, burial, etc) must be provided by the 1(1)(2)
parochial church council at its own expense.

DEPOSIT IN DRO OR RETENTION IN PAROCHIAL CUSTODY?

19 Ss.10 and 11 of the Measure contain much that was new in 1978 or 1992 and should be read with considerable

*As amended or added by the 1992 Measure.

Section of the Measure

care. They concern the use to be made of the DRO and the manner in which documents remaining in parochial custody are to be kept by their custodians.

20 The general rule is that as soon as practicable after
each periodic inspection any register whose earliest entry is 9A*
at least 150 years old at any time and which must be closed
if still in use (see paragraph 18) or which is otherwise no 10(1)(a)
longer in use and in which the last entry is 100 or more 10(2)(a)(aa)*
years old at the date when the inspection is begun must be
deposited in the appropriate DRO. Equally, records 'completed' 100 years before the same rolling date must be 10(1)(b)
deposited in that office. The diocesan bishop can however 10(2)(b)
authorise the retention in the parish of registers or records 11(3)(4)
specified by him if he is satisfied that certain standards of care will be complied with (see paragraph 23(a) below). This authorisation must be revoked in respect of any document which no longer appears to be kept to the requisite standard. Custodians are responsible for applying for authorisation to keep documents in the parish. The onus is upon them.

21 The Measure does not remove the previous right of a 10(3)
custodian of registers or records in parochial custody to deposit any of them, except current registers, in whichever is the correct DRO for the parish but the custodian must, as under the 1929 Measure, obtain the prior consent of the parochial church council. Under the 1978 Measure, however, the right to deposit extends to every custodian of such
documents, on the same terms. Any such action in 12A*
accordance with the Measure does not require a faculty.

22 There are detailed requirements in the Measure for:

(a) the supply by the depositor to the DRO and the 10(4)-(6)
bishop of:
   (i) lists of the documents being deposited, and
   (ii) lists of the documents still being retained in parochial custody after each deposit, with a statement of their usual place of custody;

*As amended or added by the 1992 Measure.

Section of the Measure

(b) the proper acknowledgement of documents by the 10(7)* DRO so that the receipt can be inserted in or annexed to the inventory of the parish concerned.

These arrangements apply whether the deposit is voluntary or mandatory (see paragraphs 20 and 21).

23. Under the 1978 Measure where documents continue in parochial custody the legal position governing their care depends on how old they are:

(a) *If they are registers whose earliest entry is at least 150 years old and which, if still in use, are subject to compulsory closure under s. 9A, or registers no longer in current use or other records all of whose contents are at least 100 years old, and if their retention has been authorised by the bishop under s.11(3)* – they must be kept in accordance with rules set out in Schedule 2 to the Measure itself and reproduced in 11(2) Appendix B of this Guide.

(b) *If they do not fall within the categories in (a) (and their retention thus needs no authorisation by the bishop)* – they are to be kept in a manner which conforms with general directions given by the bishop under s.11(6) or any supplementary directions given 11(6) by him under s.11(8). Model Directions for the 11(8) guidance of bishops when drafting their general directions under s.11(6) are included in Appendix C of this Guide (see also paragraph 24).

24 The recommended Model Directions in Appendix C are, for the most part, not binding on a diocesan bishop. However, some such directions must be given by him for the 'safekeeping, care and preservation' of all documents 11(6) coming under paragraph 23(b) above, and these must at least require that registers and records shall be housed in 11(7) the appropriate parish church or other place of public worship and must specify the type of container in which the documents are to be kept. If the bishop decides (e.g. in 11(8) view of local flooding or threat of vandalism) that supplementary directions are also necessary for a particular

*As amended or added by the 1992 Measure.

Section of the Measure

custodian or set of documents he has power to issue such further directions. They may not only add to, but also vary, his general directions so far as he thinks needful, e.g. with respect to the place of custody.

25 The bishop has *no* power, on the other hand, to vary the requirements in Schedule 2 which apply to documents coming within paragraph 23(a). However, the requirement 10(1)
to deposit such documents in the DRO unless the bishop authorises the parish to retain them under s.11(3) is a requirement to deposit the documents 'as soon as practicable' after the relevant inspection (see paragraph 20), so that in practice the deposit in the DRO could well be delayed if for any reason storage space at the repository was not immediately available.

26 The appropriate custodian remains personally 11(1)
responsible for the safety, care and preservation of documents, whether Schedule 2 or the bishop's directions apply, whether they are registers or other forms of record, and whether current or non-current. Financially, however, the parochial church council is liable for any expense involved 11(9)
in complying with Schedule 2 or the bishop's directions, whichever apply.

ENFORCEMENT BY ORDER FOR DEPOSIT

27 S.12 of the Measure imposes a duty on the bishop to act for the protection of documents held in parochial custody in certain circumstances. In any one of four situations a bishop has power to order the compulsory deposit of any such documents (except current registers):

(a) where documents falling within any of the categories 12(1)(a)
described in paragraph 23(a) have been improperly retained in the parish without the necessary authorisation under s.11(3);

(b) where that authorisation has been given for such 12(1)(b)
documents and they have not been kept to the standard of care laid down in Schedule 2;

(c) where documents less than 100 years old have not 12(1)(c)
been kept in accordance with the bishop's directions applicable to them;

Section of the Measure

(d) where for 'any other reason' documents are exposed 12(1)(d)
to danger of loss or damage.

The bishop must judge whether one of these situations has 12(1)
arisen, and if he considers that it has he must initiate the
procedure under s.12. The method whereby he determines
this is irrelevant, but if it be through the report made 12(2)
following a periodic inspection made under s.9, he must
send a copy of it to the parish custodian.

28 Before making an order the bishop is required to give 12(1)
the custodian an opportunity to make representations to
him and, unless the bishop considers the matter too urgent, 12(3)
an opportunity to rectify the situation. As under the 1929
Measure, the bishop may have recourse to the county court 12(9)
as a final means of enforcing his order.

RETURN OF DEPOSITED REGISTERS AND RECORDS

29 As was the case under the law in force prior to 1979
the fact that documents have been deposited in a DRO,
voluntarily or otherwise, does not deprive a parish of the 13(1)
right to ask the bishop for their return to parochial custody.
Before ordering their return however the bishop must be 13(2)
satisfied that the situations in paragraph 27(b) and (c) will
not exist. He must also give one month's notice to the 13(3)
DRO of the return of the documents.

CUSTODY OF REGISTERS AND RECORDS IN THE DRO

30 When any registers or records are deposited in the 14
DRO their custody (but not ownership) passes to the chief
officer of the DRO and with it all responsibility for their
'safe-keeping, care and preservation' (see paragraph 26
above). The parish custodian is released from custodial 6(4)
responsibility while the period of deposit lasts. Transfers
between DROs are permissible where diocesan boundary 15
changes or the establishment of a new DRO for part of a
diocese bring parishes into the area of a different DRO.

TEMPORARY DEPOSIT IN DRO ETC. FOR EXHIBITION OR OTHER PURPOSES

31 An extension of a 1929 provision allowing for *temporary* deposit in the DRO is to be found in s.16. It

Section of the Measure

should be given special attention. S.9 of the 1929 Measure
was available only where the deposit was needed for the
purpose of copying, and required those who wished to have
copies made to obtain the bishop's authority for deposit.
The 1978 Measure provides for temporary deposit for the 16(1)
purposes not only of copying but also of exhibition, research or listing. In addition, deposit in a suitable and safe 16(1)(4)
place, other than the DRO, if approved by the bishop after
consultation with the chief officer of the DRO, is equally in
order. Where deposit in the DRO is concerned the bishop
himself need no longer be approached unless a custodian 16(2)(3)
refuses to comply with a request for temporary deposit but
the bishop may then overrule the refusal after hearing the
views of the persons concerned. The agreement of the
parochial church council must be obtained unless the
bishop, after enquiry, overrules its refusal.

32 It should be noted that temporary deposit in a DRO 6,14
counts as deposit for the purposes of passing responsibility
for the safety of documents and for the purposes of
searches in any registers which are subject to a right of 20(2)*(3)
search.

33 A similar procedure is available whereby the chief 17(1)
officer of the DRO can authorise parish registers or records
deposited with it to be placed temporarily elsewhere, for
exhibition or research, subject to the appropriate parochial 17(3)
church council giving consent. The bishop's approval of
the place is not required in this instance, nor can he overrule the council if it refuses consent. The council itself can
obtain such a temporary deposit as of right provided the 17(2)
place chosen is suitable and safe in the judgment of the
chief officer of the DRO.

34 The maximum period for a temporary deposit in (or 18(1)
by) the DRO is initially one year but provision is made for
extension of that period.

35 Expenses of temporary deposit fall on the person 18(2)
requesting the deposit. Insurance against loss or damage 18(3)
may be insisted upon as a condition of consent to (or

*As amended or added by the 1992 Measure.

Section of the Measure

authority for) the deposit except where the parochial church council itself requests the temporary removal of its own documents from the DRO.

CARE DURING PASTORAL REORGANISATION

36 The special problems arising where parishes are dissolved (and hence the custody of their registers and records may have been transferred to a new custodian) must, subject to the provisions of the Pastoral Measure, be dealt with by specific directions of the bishop. These directions under s.19 may deal with documents of any age. 19(1)

37 Where a church is no longer used as such or is demolished, unless the bishop or a pastoral scheme directs or provides otherwise, the custodian must deposit all its registers in the DRO except current marriage registers which under s.62 of the Marriage Act 1949 should normally be forwarded to the Registrar General for formal closure. 19(2)

Searches

REGISTERS OF BAPTISMS AND BURIALS RETAINED IN THE PARISH

38 The public right of search in registers of baptism and burial while these remain in the parish was, before 1979, provided for in the Births and Deaths Registration Act 1836. The 1978 Measure incorporates the substance of this provision and extends to every custodian of these registers the right to charge fees for allowing searches and for giving certified copies, as required by the Measure, on request. The amount of each fee is laid down in the current table of parochial fees established with the approval of the General Synod under the Ecclesiastical Fees Measure 1986. A summary of the fees currently laid down (with effect from 1st January 1993) is provided in Appendix D. 20(1), 26 Sched. 4

39 By an amendment made by the 1992 Measure the right of search in these two categories of registers is limited to the extent that the custodian may require the search to be made in an authenticated photographic copy. A certificate signed by the custodian at the time the 20(3A)*

*As amended or added by the 1992 Measure.

Section of the Measure

certificate was issued is sufficient evidence of authentication. Anyone making a search who is dissatisfied with the accuracy or quality of reproduction of the photographic copy may request permission to search in the original register and the custodian may grant the facility if satisfied that the grounds are reasonable. If the custodian refuses the searcher may still refer his request to the archdeacon, and if the archdeacon is satisfied that the grounds for the request are reasonable he may direct the custodian (even if this is the DRO) to allow the original register to be searched. 20(3B)* 20(3C)*

REGISTERS OF BAPTISMS AND BURIALS DEPOSITED IN THE DRO

40 In 1979 the law changed in part with regard to searches in baptismal and burial registers which have been deposited in a DRO. Although the public right of search remains, the right of a local authority DRO (as distinct from a non-local authority DRO) to charge fees is no longer linked to those prescribed in the table of parochial fees. Under the Local Government (Records) Act 1962 the local authority controlling the DRO may charge fees for allowing inspection of records, for allowing copies to be made, or for providing copies. The amount of these fees is at the authority's discretion and, as is the common practice, it may charge no fees at all even for certified copies. If a non-local authority DRO wishes to charge fees for allowing searches it is still bound by the amounts prescribed for fees payable to the incumbent in the current table of parochial fees. (See Appendix D.) 20(2) 20(2)(b)

41 Since 1992 provision is made for the public right of search, as in the case of searches in the parish, to be limited to photocopies (see paragraph 39). The right to charge fees for such searches remains unaffected. 20(2)(3A)*-(3C)*

REGISTERS OF MARRIAGES

42 Registers of marriages remain subject to control by the State under the Marriage Act 1949. The 1978 Measure left untouched s.63 of the Act which provides for the public right of search in these registers when retained in 20(3)

*As amended or added by the 1992 Measure.

Section of the Measure

the parish. It also (as did the 1929 Measure) applies s.63 to
those marriage registers which have been deposited in the
DRO. The 1992 Measure nevertheless imposes the same 20(3A)*-
limitations on the right of search in pre-1837 marriage (3C)*
registers as on baptismal and burial registers (see paragraphs 39 and 41). (Details of the fees payable for searches in the register of marriages and for marriage certificates are given in Appendix D.)

DESTINATION OF FEES

43 A DRO is not required to account to the incumbent or 20(4)
any other former custodian for any fees in respect of searches in his deposited registers.

WAIVER OF FEES

44 The position with regard to the reduction or waiver of fees is explained in Appendix D.

Miscellaneous

45 The remaining provisions of the 1978 Measure concern the recovery of registers in the possession of un- 21-27
authorised persons, certain duties of a DRO in connection with marriage registers, and other miscellaneous matters which need only be studied by those requiring to know every detail of the Measure. It may be helpful to be reminded, however, that though the Measure received Royal Assent in 1978 it came into operation on 1st January 1979, the date which the Archbishops had determined in accordance with s.27. Similarly, it should be noted that although 27(2)
the latest Amending Measure, namely the Church of
England (Miscellaneous Provisions) Measure 1992, was 1992
given Royal Assent on 6th March 1992 the Archbishops by Measure
a determination in accordance with s.19(2) of the 1992 19(2)
Measure have arranged that its relevant provisions shall come into operation on 1st January 1993.

*As amended or added by the 1992 Measure.

APPENDIX B

Schedule 2 to the Measure*

(Provisions which apply to register books and records retained in parochial custody under section 11(3))

1 Every register book or record to which this Schedule applies shall be kept in a wood-lined, rust-proofed, vented steel cabinet, the door of which is fitted with a multi-lever lock or in a fire-proofed muniment room conforming so far as practicable to British Standard Specification Number 5454 or any new British Standard which supersedes it.

2 The cabinet or muniment room shall be situated within the appropriate parish church or other place of public worship, positioned where there is least risk of damage to any such book or record in the event of a flood or an outbreak of fire, and made secure in all other respects against flood, fire and theft.

3 The temperature and relative humidity in such cabinet or muniment room shall be checked at least once a week by means of a maximum-minimum thermometer and a hygrometer, each of which shall be kept in the cabinet or muniment room. Records of all readings shall be kept for a period of not less than twelve months and be made available for inspection at any reasonable time by the archdeacon in whose archdeaconry the parish is situated or by such person or persons as he may appoint.

4 The hygrometer shall be one conforming to British Standard Specification Number 3292 or any new British Standard which supersedes it.

5 The temperature in the cupboard or muniment room shall not be allowed to rise above 18 degrees Celsius and the difference between the maximum and minimum temperatures during any week shall not be allowed to exceed 10 degrees Celsius.

6 The relative humidity in the cupboard or muniment room shall not be allowed to fall below 50 per cent or to rise above 65 per cent.

7 Subject to paragraph 3 above, nothing, except books or other documents, shall be kept in the cupboard or muniment room in which

*As amended by the Church of England (Miscellaneous Provisions) Measure 1992 s.4, and Sched. 1, para. 12.

any register book or record to which this Schedule applies is for the time being kept.

8 Without prejudice to the preceding provisions, the person or persons having the custody of any such book or record shall take all such steps as are reasonably practicable to ensure that the book or record is protected against theft, loss and damage.

Note: The 'cupboard' referred to in paras 5, 6 and 7 above is the same as the 'cabinet' of paras 1, 2 and 3.

APPENDIX C

Model Directions for Bishops under Section 11(6)

(applicable to registers and records under 100 years old)

Application

1 These directions apply to:

(a) the register books of baptisms, confirmations, banns of marriage, marriages, burials and services provided for any parish church or other place of public worship in a parish; and
(b) other parochial records, that is to say, materials in written or other form setting out facts or events or otherwise recording information which are in the custody of the incumbent or priest in charge or of churchwardens or of the parochial church council or in the joint custody of any of them;

except any register book or record to which Schedule 2 to the Parochial Registers and Records Measure 1978 applies by virtue of s.11(2) of that Measure.

2 The register books and other parochial records to which these directions apply are hereinafter referred to as 'books and records'.

Safe-keeping, Care, etc.

3 When not in use by any minister of the parish concerned or by any other person authorised in that behalf by the parochial church council of that parish the books and records shall be kept in a container which affords as much protection against theft, damp, rust and vermin as is reasonably practicable, and unless the bishop otherwise directs under s.11(8) of the Parochial Registers and Records Measure 1978 the container shall be kept in the appropriate parish church or other place of public worship. In this paragraph 'minister', in relation to a parish, means the incumbent of a benefice to which the parish belongs, a vicar in a team ministry for the area of that benefice, the priest in charge of the parish and any curate licensed to officiate in the parish.

4 The place in which the container is kept shall be:

(a) a place which is well ventilated and likely to remain dry and in which the temperature is unlikely to vary greatly during any period of 24 hours; and

(b) the place where there is least risk of damage to the books and records in the event of flood or an outbreak of fire.

5 The container should be opened to air the contents for at least half an hour about once a week, on a dry day, not a wet one.

6 No objects or materials other than the registers and records should be kept in the container. (It is especially important that nothing can by leakage or melting leave stains on the documents.)

7 No person having the custody of any book or record shall allow any other person to remove it from the church or other place in which it is kept unless he is empowered or required to do so by any statutory provision and, in particular, by a provision of the Parochial Registers and Records Measure 1978 or an order made thereunder.

8 Where the person having the custody of any book or record allows another person to make a search in it, the custodian or his representative shall remain in attendance throughout the search with a view to ensuring that the book or record is not damaged or stolen.

9 (1) Where it appears to the incumbent or priest in charge of the benefice to which a parish belongs that the books and records may be exposed to additional risk of damage or loss by reason of the fact:

(a) that the parish is likely to be dissolved by a pastoral scheme; or

(b) that it is likely that a church or other place of public worship in the parish will, by reason of a declaration of redundancy, demolition or otherwise, cease to be used as such;

he shall ask the archdeacon in whose archdeaconry the parish is to advise him as to the steps he should take in order to ensure the safe-keeping of the books and records.

(2) During a vacancy in a benefice when no priest in charge has been appointed, the duty imposed by sub-paragraph (1) above on the incumbent or priest in charge shall be discharged by the churchwardens of the parish affected.

APPENDIX D

Notes on Search and Certificate Fees

Amounts of Fees Payable

1 The following are relevant extracts from tables of fees laid down by the Parochial Fees Order 1992 (S.I. 1992 No. 1747 – in force from 1st January 1993) and details of certain fees payable under Acts of Parliament. Both categories of fees are revised from time to time. Current information can be obtained from the Church Commissioners at 1 Millbank, London SW1P 3JZ and the Registrar General at Smedley Hydro, Trafalgar Road, Birkdale, Southport PR8 2HH respectively.

2 It should especially be noted that an incumbent or parochial church council is entitled to a fee under the Parochial Fees Order only where the register remains in parochial custody. Under s.20 of the 1978 Measure, no fees under the Order are payable to the incumbent or parochial church council for searches or copy entries in the case of registers which have been deposited in a DRO. As to the fees payable in respect of deposited registers, see paragraphs 7 and 8.

EXTRACTS FROM THE 1992 ORDER

	Fee payable to Incumbent £
Searching[1] registers of marriages prior to 1837[2] (up to 1 hour)	5.00 (2.00*)
(each subsequent hour or part of an hour)	3.00 (2.00*)
Searching[1] registers of baptisms or burials (including provision of one copy[3] of any entry therein) (up to one hour)	5.00 (2.00*)
(for each subsequent hour or part of an hour)	3.00 (2.00*)

[1] The Parochial Fees Order provides that the search fee prescribed by the Order relates to a 'particular search' where the approximate date of the baptism, marriage or burial is known. The Order also provides that the fees for a more general search would be negotiable with the incumbent and parochial church council.

[2] No fee is currently payable for the period after 1836.

[3] Although this provision of the Parochial Fees Order does not specifically refer to a certified copy, s.20 of the 1978 Measure imposes an obligation to provide such a copy on request and on payment of any prescribed fee.

* An additional fee payable to the parochial church council.

Each additional copy of any entry in a register of baptisms or burials	5.00 (2.00*)
Certificate of baptism issued at time of baptism	5.00
Short certificate of baptism given under s.2, Baptismal Registers Measure 1961	3.00
Certificate of banns (of marriage) issued at time of publication	5.00
Certificate of burial issued at time of burial[4]	5.00

FEES PAYABLE UNDER VARIOUS ACTS OF PARLIAMENT[5]

Certificate of marriage:	
at registration	2.00
subsequently	5.50
(s.63, Marriage Act 1949)	
For each entry in the incumbent's quarterly return to the superintendent registrar of entries made in the marriage register (s.57(4), Marriage Act 1949)	1.30
Certificate of marriage for certain purposes (s.10, Savings Bank Act 1887, and s.160(2), Social Security Act 1975)	1.50
Certificate of name altered or given in baptism (s.13(2), Births and Deaths Registration Act 1953)	1.00

Payment for Assistance beyond the Course of Duty

3 No statutory fee is payable unless the custodian of a register is legally bound to grant facilities or to render assistance in connection with it. For example he is not bound:

(a) to permit the photographing of the register;
(b) to supply certificates on postal application;
(c) to make searches on behalf of an enquirer;
(d) to produce a copy of any register where the original has been deposited in the DRO.

---

[4] No fee is payable in respect of the burial of a still-born infant or an infant dying within the period of one year after birth.

[5] Current amounts are in accordance with the Registration of Births, Marriages and Deaths (Fees) Order 1992 (S.I. 1992 No. 99), in force from 1st April 1992.

* An additional fee payable to the parochial church council.

He may however consent to give such assistance, on terms to be agreed between himself and the enquirer, in connection with either registers or *records*. These terms may include remuneration and/or expenses.

Waiver of Fees

4 The Church Commissioners are currently revising the 'Guide to Church of England Fees'. The following notes may be found helpful meanwhile.

5 From time to time an incumbent or parochial church council may feel that all or part of a fee should be waived. As to this, the following should, please, be borne in mind:

(a) Fees established by the Parochial Fees Order are imposed under a Measure (the Ecclesiastical Fees Measure 1986) which has the same force as an Act of Parliament; the Order itself has been approved by the General Synod and submitted to Parliament. So the fees are legally payable.

(b) If an incumbent waives his fees the diocese will in most cases have to find additional funds to bring his stipend to an agreed level. Ultimately these extra funds will have to be provided via the quota; *so the effect is that the laity of the diocese in general will bear the cost.* This consideration applies to *all fees*, even if they are not prescribed by Parochial Fees Orders.

So any departure, as a general rule, from the practice of collecting fees would be undesirable.

6 If it is nevertheless felt for a pastoral reason (e.g. the funeral of a young child who was one year of age or over), that a fee or charge should on a particular occasion be waived or reduced, regard should be had to any guidelines laid down by the diocese, and the agreement of both the incumbent and the parochial church council should be obtained where both are entitled to receive a part of the sum in question. It is recommended that parochial church councils should in general delegate their rights of waiver to incumbents, but on the understanding that an incumbent will report to a council on any fees waived on its behalf.

Registers deposited in DROs

REGISTERS OF BAPTISMS AND BURIALS

7 When deposited in a DRO controlled by a local authority these are (since 1979) no longer subject to the tables of fees in the Parochial Fees

Orders. Nevertheless s.20 of the Parochial Registers and Records Measure 1978 makes it clear that a local authority DRO still has the right to charge fees, both for searches and for certified copies of entries, in these two registers. The continuing right stems from s.1 of the Local Government (Records) Act 1962. But it is a right not an obligation. Non-local authority DROs may, at their discretion, charge the same fees for permitting searches and providing certified copies of entries in deposited baptism and burial registers as would be payable under the Parochial Fees Orders to an incumbent (but not to a parochial church council).

REGISTERS OF MARRIAGES

8 If deposited in *any* DRO these also (in 1979) ceased to be subject to the Parochial Fees Orders but they are subject to s.63 of the Marriage Act 1949. S.63 does not now prescribe a fee for a *search* by a member of the public. However, the fee for a *certificate* given under s.63 of the Marriage Act continues to be payable. A local authority DRO also has the right to charge a fee under s.1 of the Local Government (Records) Act 1962 for a search in a marriage register of a date prior to 1837, as in the case of a baptismal or burial register.

Destination of Fees payable during a Vacancy

9 During a vacancy in a benefice, fees which, but for the vacancy, would be paid to the incumbent should be paid to the diocesan board of finance or to such other person as the board, after consultation with the bishop, may direct (Ecclesiastical Fees Measure 1986 s.3(1)).

APPENDIX E
Notes on Parochial Libraries

1 Before about 1680, a modest number of libraries had been established in parochial custody, principally in market towns, and these were often intended for the use of citizens and clergy alike. After 1680 many libraries were founded in those churches where the poorer incumbents were unlikely to possess their own bookstock. Many such libraries were founded through the initiative of Dr Thomas Bray and subsequently by the efforts of the Associates of Dr Bray. These libraries were regulated by an Act passed in 1708 for the *Better Preservation of Parochial Libraries in England.* Its provisions include the compilation of a library catalogue, its deposit in the diocesan registry, and the maintenance of a register of benefactors. It refers to the responsibility of the churchwardens in securing the library during a vacancy. The Act should be viewed in the context of the parochial library movement of the early eighteenth century, but it is important to note that the legislation is still operative. It stipulates that no books should be alienated without the consent of the Ordinary (the diocesan chancellor), and this provision is reinforced by the Faculty Jurisdiction Measure 1964, which requires that the advice of the diocesan advisory committee should be sought in such cases. Later in the eighteenth century, there was a marked decline in the foundation of libraries. However many small parochial lending libraries were founded in the nineteenth century by the SPCK.

2 In 1959, a committee of the Central Council for the Care of Churches, appointed to investigate the number and condition of parochial libraries of the Church of England, produced a report entitled *The Parochial Libraries of the Church of England*, which included an alphabetical list of all known libraries founded by the mid-nineteenth century, and a copy of the Act of 1708. The report recommended that only in exceptional circumstances should parishes dispose of such collections. Care should also be taken to preserve libraries of more recent origin. The 1959 report was not primarily concerned with *liturgica* and books acquired for example as a result of legal requirements. It recommended that 'unless circumstances absolutely forbid, a parochial library ought to be retained in its own home'. Its authors nevertheless envisaged that if a parish was no longer able to maintain its library the books might need to be transferred to another library in the vicinity. Since 1959, a number of parochial libraries have been deposited on loan in cathedral, university, or public libraries or in the appropriate DRO with parish registers and records.